STEP ZERO

SOLUTION TO PROBLEMS OF FIRST
VENTURE, LEARN HOW TO INVEST ZERO
TO GO RICH, YOU DO NOT NEED MONEY TO
GO RICH AFTER THIS

ANUJ BHARADWAJ

This book is dedicated to first-time founders only.

I am going to share my own experience and

what I learned from my mentors.

This book will help first-time

founders/New Entrepreneurs in

their first venture.

Contents

Preface

Why step zero?
    When I was studying at college.
    I learned about the law of thermodynamics.
    This law was more important than the first law.
    Hence scientists accepted this law as
    zeroth law of thermodynamics.
    I derived this name *step zero* from there.
    This book will act as a pillar of your
    business and life as well.
    During our school days what we learned ,
    10 is greater than 9,11 is greater than 10.
    zero is the smallest number.
    This is true in theory but not in
    business, investing, and finance.
    we think this because we learned this
    in school. we have memories
    of this since childhood.
    In real life, It may or may not be true.
    compare 10 bucks 10 years
    and 11 bucks today.
    Do you still think 11 is
    greater than 10 now?
    Of course not.
    If your compare 500 bucks 30 years
    before and 40,000 bucks in present day
    what you think ?which will be greator ?
    This is how people are going poor
    but still happy because they see
    a big number in form of earned income.
    What my Journey taught me is

The biggest number which will help
you in your Journey is zero.
Every time you get zero
you will become a better version of yourself.
Let us see some practical examples
to understand this well.
If your cost per acquisition of customers is *zero*
your business will be a big business one day.
If you can start a business with *zero investment*
from your pocket, you can do business easily.
You do not need money to make money.
If you want to start a business and
do not have money to start a business
then it is a golden opportunity.
Start your journey now. Once
you started a
business without money it
will become your habit to start
business without money and those
who has money in hand to start
Businesses are very unlucky because
it will become their habit.
They need money to start any business.
So, Even if you have money to
start a business,I recommend to not use
the money to start the business.
In this way you will invest zero to
start your first venture.
People like to have property,Money etc
in their own name but they forget one thing.
Robbers will rob you,if you have money.
Dacoit will force fully take precious
thing or money from you,if you have.

World will be with you if you
have money,Property etc.
you are at risk.
you will never know that
who are really with you
if you property or money.
So,Have nothing in your name.
Keep everything with your
coorporation's name.
You control your coorporation.
you control the property,money etc.
This is why rich people have nothing
and enjoy everthing which they want.
No one can impose tax on them
because they have nothing.
No one can rob them.
Noone can take anything from them.

I

Introduction

First-time founders are the most important
asset for any country and Society.
First-time founders will give shape to the future
of the economy of a country or Society.
Yes, it is hard. It is tough. It is even impossible
for those who lack Entrepreneurial Spirit.
Only those people who are entrepreneurs
by heart and soul will survive.
The remaining will leave this
journey because it is very painful.
Remember entrepreneurship is a Journey.
It has no destiny. We just cross the
next milestone again and again.
So,Get ready to face pain which
everyone cannot tolerate.
you will listen no everyday.
you will fail everyday.
This is very common in Entreprenureship.
So be comfortable being uncomfortable
and start the hardest journey of your life.

II

Identity

Before starting my Journey
    what I generally think
    "From where do people arrange
    funds to start a Big business".
    Do they earn money and then
    establish the business. I was not
    even aware of the existence
    of investors. But I often
    think how can I get so much
    the fund so that I can also
    establish a big business.
    During my Journey, I get
    information about investors
    from my first mentor.
    who is a real estate investor?
    But, I modified this so that
    you can understand it easily.
    There are two types of investors.
    1. Insider Investors
    2. Outsider Investor

Insider Investor

When we begin our Journey
we have no money and no knowledge.
This is *Step Zero i.e* you are at *step zero.*
we know just myths taught by
people who have no knowledge
about business or investing.
But they gave us advice in such a way that
"It seems that they have huge knowledge
about business and investing". Still, they are poor.
They will tell you business is risky.
My mentor taught me business means risk management
I like to tell you that Business means Risk elimination.
When other people are poor they
stay in their comfort zone.
So, They remain poor till the end of their life.
The next generation does the same as well.
When we are poor we leave
our comfort zone to get rich.
To achieve that objective we
incorporate corporations.
We start a business with a specific mission.
We get surplus cash as a side product of the business.
Remember, This will not happen in just the first attempt.
But when it happens, It will change your life forever.
In this way, you became an insider investor.
So, when you have no money.
you start a business to get surplus cash
then you became an insider investor.
Remember, You are a real investor.
Those who are poor invest in the Share market,

Mutual funds, Pension funds, etc, and in this way,
people like us get control over their money.
we use their money to grow our business and go rich.
They bear all the tax burden and we give them a
return on their investment as per our norms.
In this way, they became gamblers.
This breed of gamblers is known as retail investors.

<u>Outsider investors</u>

When you get surplus cash you may invest
that surplus cash in other businesses.
To go rich further. When you were an
insider investor you learned a lot about
business. This knowledge will help you to
decide in which business you shall
invest and in which business you shall not invest.
You shall do so because it is scalable.
You cannot run hundreds of businesses.
But you can invest in hundreds
or thousands of Businesses.
Now, You are an Outsider investor.
You just invested in a good business.
You are not the founder of the business.
Now, the question is why other
people cannot do so and go rich.
The answer is very simple.
Security exchange board or any other
equivalent organization
favor people like us. They do not allow other
people to invest in those investments.
This is not only a conspiracy of the rich.
You will know more about conspiracy

when you will be part of this ecosystem.
So, First-time founders/New Entrepreneurs
are insider investors.
*I recommend you to be an outsider
investor after 8 - 10 years of experience at least.
So, Ultimately we started our
journey from *step zero.*
This is why *step zero* is important.
If we do not reach *step zero,*
we cannot start our journey.
When you get your first success,
you crossed *step Zero.*
After this, you will reach
step 1, Step 2, Step 3, etc.
Once you learn how to take this *step zero* you can
take steps 1, Step 2,..... etc easily.
Now, outsider investors are of many types
1. Seed funds
2. Angel investors
3. Micro Venture Capitalist
4. Venture Capitalists
5.Private equity(PE) investors

III

Corporation

Every game has a set of rules.
    The rules of our game are known as the law.
    So, you need to understand some sections
    of the law which will help you a lot.
    Hence you shall find legal structure which shall
    1.Limit your liability
    2. your Corporation can get investment
    via maximum methods
    like investment from variours investors
    investment from public like Bonds,IPO
    Investment from Banks like Loans etc
    If you cannot get investment from all
    then can you convert the coorporation
    to another legal entity to get fund
    from every legal method in future.
    3.your coorporation can be sold if required ?
    You may or may not sell in future
    but you need such legal entity
    which can be sold,if required in future.
    4.your budget

Even after incorporation you need to
take care of compliance.
5.Do more research to find out if
I missed something else which
is essential.

IV
Funding

This *step zero* will teach you
everything you need to go rich.
Step zero is your best teacher.
Zero People will help you in *step zero*.
you will get *zero investment* in *step zero*.
Now, you may ask me" what shall
we invest in this *step zero*".
The answer is very simple. Invest this zero.
This is the beauty of rich people.
They search for ways to invest
even if they have no money.
I learn this from my experience which
I am going to share with you.
This framework will help you
to raise funds at *Step Zero*.
When I tried to raise funds for
my first company Excellloans Pvt Ltd
I get multiple failures.
I tried to raise funds from friends.
I tried to raise funds from banks.

I tried to raise funds from Investors.
I failed every time.
My friend told me that he will invest but did
agree later on during the time of investment.
My relative who are bankers, I contacted them.
They did not receive my call after that.
My elder brother told to her wife in front
of me"He cannot do business because
he does not have money".
Everyone broke my heart, but I did not
give up because of both of my mentors.
What I learned from both of my mentors
is that *you do not need money to make money.*
I know that there is some way to do so
I just need to find out the correct method.
After three to six months my brother tell me
some harsh words in front of my mother
due to which my mother gave me some
golden jewelry so that I can do something.
Later on, I discovered to start any business
people like our family members, friends, and relative
become our first investors. This is how we start the
business.

After a year my business did not grow.
But I invested most of my money but
my business did not grow still. I did some
experiments so that I can get a source
of income. I buy a new laptop, hard disk,
and Internet connection but the
experiment failed again.
The cost of this failure was 63k.
But I get some assets at least.
So the very first thing you need to

do is to create a source of Income
for your business after getting the first funding.
Do not do the mistakes that I did.
This source of income shall be substantial
and the product/service which you are
promoting shall be a low-ticket Item.
If possible, start creating that
product or service right now
and test it after providing this
to the first 10 customers for free.
Remember to improve this product
or service quarter by quarter or year by year.
Remember you need to sell it even if it is free.
This is called MVP(Minimum viable product)
This shall be the first impression
of your business on customers.
If your product is not a good
MVP then create another.

Features of MVP

This product shall be designed in
such a way that people shall be your fans.
This first product shall give information
about your product or service in such
a way that people can use your product
or service without much struggle.
Give as much value as possible.
There is one more method to raise funds.
People will get ready to pay
you money if you do
some work for them.
I mean a part-time job or

some other source of earning.
Don't think that you are
working for money or a paycheck.
Use every buck for your business only.
You are raising funds for your venture.
You may ask how much time you need so.
I recommend continuing
this process to raise funds
till your business crossed the first
million in revenue and
your business has attended the stage
of the compound effect.
Please confirm that what you are
doing is in accordance with the law.
This part-time job and working
as a founder, co-founder, etc shall be
in accordance with the law.
Now you may ask what about investors?
The answer is very simple.
Investors will not invest in you.
Investors invest in a business
with good systems.
Yes, They invest in systems.
Not on people.
When you create such systems
you have a very unfair advantage
to deal with investors.
Cash is a liability. Inflation is
eating their money.
They have to invest in order
to grow their money.
When they find a good system
they have to invest in otherwise they will

face a loss due to inflation.
But at this stage, why not opt for debt?
If you opt for a debt you do not have
to dilute share/ownership of your company.
ROI for debt is lesser than ROI
which investors demand.
Then why not opt for debt?
I am still searching for answers to this question.
***Remember to work on facts and
data from now, not on guesses.***
I have created a framework
that will help you take the decision
for fundraising at step zero.
1. Cost of the fund shall be zero.
2. You do not have to return funds after raising.
3. Those people who love you more
than their money
and have surplus money/ good
in the management of money will help you.
When you succeed you will help them as well.
There is one more method
that my mentor says often.
Learn how to sell and do
real estate business.
You will easily get into
debt in the real estate business.
But beware, because debt may
help you to grow if you have good knowledge.
But, it may wipe out you if you did any mistake.
This is why I did not get involved
in the real estate business
as I know I cannot handle debt
as I do not have enough knowledge now.

Now, you do not need money
to start any business.
Even if you have, I recommend not
using that money for business purposes.
Raise funds and invest them in your business.
Every time you raise funds
you will be a better version of yourself.
Now you do not need money to do any business.
Funding Rounds through which
companies raise funds are
Pre-seed
Seed Fund
Series A
Series B
Series C
When I started my company
I was thinking that what
other founders are doing due
to which they are getting funding
and what mistake I am doing due to
which I am not getting investment?
Later on, I saw a video on YT channel of
YC combinator and understand that
rarely the first-time founders get funding.
Later on, in an event that a Micro VC told
us "In the USA there are some funds which
Focus only on Failed Founders".
So, if you are failed founder still you
may get funding. It is not a bad thing for them.
One more thing which I like to share
with you which I learned from
other Entrepreneurs-
Investors will invest in the business

for growth only. If your business is not growing
then it is quite hard to get funding.
One more thing you need to take care.
All investors are not same.
You may find some investors which
are not active investors.
They may meet you just because
they want to show off that
they are rich or which know
many people who are rich and popular.
Beware of those investors.
Only reason to invest in your
company is because you are
going to create a great company.
It is not personal.
So,approach only active investors.
Specially,if you can find a founder
who have sold his/her business
recently then you may get investment soon.

V
Solutions

After this chapter, you will be able
    to find solutions to every problem
    in your life and business as well.
    After six years of journey, I understand
    one thing which is very Amazing.
    This one concept will
    change your life forever.
    "Solution to every question and
    answer to every question in your life
    or business is available in your inner world.
    The outer world is just
    a reflection of your inner world"
    So, next time you have any
    problem or question remember to
    Search for answers in your inner world.
    Let us see how you can do so.
    I learned this concept after six years
    of my Journey which is very Amazing.
    You need to understand people at three levels

1. Desire centric People
2. Problem centric People
3. Solution centric People

1. **Desire-centric People**: People who have the
desire to achieve something are desire-centric.
They have no idea about problems or solutions.
They don't even know that some problem is there.
They just have a desire and
everyone starts from this stage.
If you listen to their language
you will clearly understand that
somehow he wanted to
achieve some desire.
When I started my journey
my desire was to be Ultra rich.
I was thinking that
"I can do anything if I have money".
Before starting the company
I approached Investors, banks, etc.
After some years of struggle,
I discovered that money is not the problem.
2. **Problem-Centric People**: People who know
about problems and looking for
the solution to the problem is
Problem centric People.
If you will listen to their word you will
see clearly understand that they are facing
some problems but they do
not know the solution.
During my Journey, I understand to
achieve my desire that I need to be
a big business owner to be Ultra Rich.

But I was not aware that how can I do so.
How can I be Big Business Owner?
3. **Solution-Centric People:** People who have knowledge
about Problems, Solutions both
are Solution Centric People.
They know that their
desire is a side product.
Many times you will listen to
some Entrepreneurs, say
"Money is a side product"
They are solution-centric people.
They know the more problems
they face smarter they will be.
Now let us understand four types of People
I learned this from my first mentor
who is a successful real estate investor.
1. Employees:
2. Self-employed:
3. Big Business owner:
4. Investors
Everyone has their own distinct character.
You need to understand every kind of person.

Employee

These are people who work for job security.
They pay 50% of their earned income in taxes.
They are trained by our education
system to be an employee.
They became part of the system and works
with the rules and regulations of the system.
They earn if they work.
They do not earn if they do not work.
They work for a salary.

Self-employed or small business owner

They are themself a system.
They are perfectionists.
They are good at sales.
They like to work in their own way.
They do not like to obey the orders of other people.
Basically, They find jobs for them.
Then they work on that job.
People like celebrities, Practicing Professionals
like Doctors, CA, CS, small businesses, etc
fall into this category.
They pay 60 % of their money in taxes.
They also have no financial knowledge.
They earn if they work.
They do not earn if they do not work.
They are solo players and think
that if you want to do anything
perfect then do it yourself.
They work for Money.

<u>Big Business owner</u>

They are system owners.
Their business works even without their presence.
They earn even if they do not work.
They have excellent financial knowledge.
They create businesses that can raise funds by various means.
Their trained by their rich mentors, their mistakes, their journey of entrepreneurship, etc.
Problems are opportunities for these kinds of people.
The more problems they face, the smarter they became.
The bigger problems they face stronger they became.
Their mistakes are their best lesson.
Failure is their best teacher.
In their world money is not a problem.

Having surplus money is the problem.

They have nothing on paper but virtually they control everything.

They pay 0% to 20% in taxes.

They are team players.

They do not work for money.

If you want to get rich, you need to be a big business owner.

Investors

Investors are also Entrepreneurs.

Investors are people who invest in

the system created by Big Business Owners.

Money is their commodity.

They also have excellent financial knowledge.

They pay 0 % in taxes.

They do not want to take control

or overtake your business.

They want their desired returns.

They are outsider investors.

Now, Look into your inner world.

You will succeed only when you became

a solution-centric and big business owner.

Even If you are not there, it's ok.

With time and consistent effort, you can do so.

But I like to give you the shortest path to reach there.

VI

Path

It took years for me to learn this concept.
  When I was 14 years old, A girl came into my life.
  In the beginning, we fought a lot.
  But with time we fall in love with each other.
  When it happened I do not know.
  She proposed to me via various methods.
  she proposed to me by writing a love letter.
  I enjoyed her effort.
  I confirmed that she is the girl but
  she never approached me directly.
  At that time my dream was to be
  an Army officer in the Indian Army.
  My plan was to be an Army officer
  first so that her father and family shall
  agree with our relationship.
  But I forget about the most important part
  i.e accepting her love. I became a good student then.
  I tries hard but failed to pass the written
  competitive exam for an Indian Army officer.
  I tries again and failed again.

I forget my love now and tried hard to
be an Indian Army officer often.
I never passed the written competitive exam.
In between, I got news of her death.
I did not believe it for the first six months.
I searched for her everywhere.
I even went to her friend's house
directly and ask upfront about her. Finally,
I accepted the reality that she is no more.
Finally, learned and decided to live
with her dream till the end of my life.
This was the last happiness of my life
but soon I was going to lose that also.
After several years my Mother faced an accident.
But thank god" she survived".
I already lost my love.
I can not afford to lose anyone else.
On that day I came from the wedding
of one of my neighbors.
I did not take a rest that night and my mother
faced that accident in the Morning.
I did not sleep for the next five nights as well.
Her backbone get a minor fracture
in the accident and the doctor
told her to get complete bed rest for two months.
What I was thinking before the accident
is"My mother and father
will take care of everything or my elder
brother and her wife will
take responsibility" and I will remain free.
I will not marry for several years.
After some years no girl will marry me.
No father will accept me as the

life partner of her daughter.
After this accident, my emotions changed.
My brother came after a month after the accident.
My brother's wife came five months after the accident.
I look after my mother but I am a boy and she is a woman.
There is a limitation.
My father is a purohit.
He went to the temple every morning
because Money is also important.
Now, I was thinking
"There is no one who can take care of my parents.
There is no one who can take care of my house.
There is no one with whom I can
Share the emotions of my heart"
My sister helps us a lot in that need of the hour.
She told me" if you do not sleep you will also fall sick".
when my brother-in-law went out of the station
my sister send me to her house to sleep during the night.
Next, five-night was very transformative for my life.
Now, Two kinds of feelings are coming into my mind.
1. I have to leave my last happiness
2. How can I do so? I cannot.
Again
1. Leave her dreams now. You need to marry.
2. How can I do so? I cannot
On the fifth night, I got the solution that I read in
a Book "*Atomic Habits by James Clear*"
Look at the two statements again.
These are not two sentences.
These are two sentences by two different
identities inside my inner world.
Both are fighting for their survival.

One is the future husband of someone.
Another is the lover of a girl who is no more.
Everything became normal when the lover
in my inner world lost their existence.
The problem was not that my love died.
Problem was that the lover inside me remains alive.
The same is applicable to every Entrepreneur.
I learned this concept from the book *E-myth.*
There are three kinds of people in any business
1. Executive
2. Manager
3. Entrepreneur
These three identities are
fighting for their survival.
The executive always thinks that
the company/superiors want to
get maximum work from them.
Managers are people who work and
take decisions on their past experience.
An entrepreneur is a person
who lives in the future.
In our inner world, all these identities are
fighting with each other for their survival.
Our business will grow only when
entrepreneurs in our inner world
will exist and remanning all Identities
to lose their existence.

Look at the photos.
Both of the photos are my photo.
But identities are different.
The boy on the left-hand side is the lover.
The boy on the right-hand side is a boy
who is the future husband of a girl?
This transformation is due to a change in identity.
I get this result in just 1 to 2 months.
People were shocked to see this transformation
in such a small interval of time.
You will also shock to know that this
transformation is a side product.
The main product is a change in identity.
"Now if you face any trouble in your life,
please search for answers
inside your inner world. The outer world is
just a reflection of our inner world."
Process
If you want to get any flowers, fruit, vegetable,

or anything with the commercial value
you need to follow some specific process.
But if you want to get weeds or Jungle bushes
no Process is required.

.

This is applicable in our life as well.
If you want to be a person with high value
then you need to follow a specific process.
If you want to be a rich person you need
to follow some specific process.
If you do not change your identity and process
then there will be no change in your life.
So, Search for the right process you need.
It may be correct or incorrect on
the first attempt but do not worry.
keep trying till you reached to correct process.
Please remember time and consistency
is a key element of any process.
So, It will take time and you need to
be consistent in the process.
When I joined the gym I used
the same formula again.
I created a new identity in my inner world.
Now I am an Athlete, a Gymmer.
This identity is just my thinking that
"From today I am an Athlete, a Gymmer."
So, what is the process?
I go to the gym every day, even when
I am not feeling well as well.
Do work out for 60 minutes to 90 minutes.
I repeat the same activity every day except Sunday.
What result do I get?
I lift 130 kg four days a week in the gym.

I am planning to lift 150 kg in the future.
But it is just a side product.
The main product is my identity and process.
If you keep the focus on identity and process
you will automatically get the desired result.
If you are not getting the desired result then
something is wrong with your identity or process.
What people do is focus on changing results
but do not focus on identity and process.
Hence, they face a huge struggle to achieve success.
So here is the ultimate formula for success
(1)Identity or thinking - (2)Process -(3)Result
Remember identity and process
are in your hands, not the result.
So focus on the first two.
Do not worry about the results.
If your identity and process are correct
you will get the desired result.
If not then check your identity and process.
When I Entered the world of Business,
What I think is "I am smart Enough".
Every time I implement my own
strategy, I fail badly.
Again I create another strategy, I fail again.
I try my best to succeed, but I failed.
It was very tough, I was very frustrated.
I often think shall I give up and
get another Job?
Again, I think that no I will
continue my Journey.
I failed in my first venture.
I failed in my second venture.
I failed in my third venture.

It was very very frustrating for me.
But when I joined Gym.
I get Amazing results in
just one to two months.
Then, I asked my third Mentor
who is my Gym trainer.
How much time is required to
get this result generally?
What he replied shocked me.
He replied"one year".
Again I started thinking.
How did I get this success?
I did something which I am
unable to understand.
Yes, my Identity is a major factor.
But something else is also there which
I am unable to understand.
After some days I was thinking
"is it due to the mentorship of my third mentor? "
(My mentor has more than
two years of experience in the Gym)
We know each other from class six(6).
He gave me professional training
for two months and I did not even know
names of all workouts in the Gym
but I perform every day.
I implemented the same
strategies on youtube
and guess what "I succeeded".
One more thing is common in both cases
(in the case of gym and Youtube)
In the very first month, I go to
Gym and paid for the first month.

The gym owner told me that
"I have to pay for admission fee separately"
I paid the admission fee on the third day.
In the case of youtube, I paid for the course in which
I get the information about the strategy to be used
in youtube.
With time I recognized that
"Except identity and process"
There are some secondary factors as well.
You need to learn proven Processes.
You need to pay for that proven process.
You need to test the proven process at a small level.
Then increase the level when the process is working smoothly.
This is my proven process to do anything.

VII
Productivity

Since childhood, I hesitate to say "*no*"
    to my Parents, brothers, sister, friends, Relatives,
    Neighbors just because they praise me.
    I hesitate to say no to anyone, even strangers.
    Even when I say no my parents force me
    to say yes to many things.
    Even if I resist still people force me
    a little and I agree with them.
    But what happened after the accident
    of my Mother.
    I forcefully denied everyone.
    I do not know why I am doing so.
    I just do not want to engage in
    work that is not my business.
    Then I joined Gym.
    I just focus on Gym.
    When I completed my professional
    training in Gym .For three months
    I do not focus on anything else.
    After the third month, I focused on

youtube, I get success.
Now I can rank videos on youtube.
Yes, I continued to do workouts in Gym
but worked on youtube as well.
After two continuous success
what I found in my research is
going to help me in every project
in my life.
One person can focus on just one thing
at a time or a maximum of two things.
If you like to do all work together
you will not be able to do anything.
So, Work on one thing at a time.
Learn to say no.
Focus on only those things which
is essential for you because
if you will not succeed you
cannot do anything for anyone.
But if you succeed you can help
anyone you want to help.
Secondly, Learn to plan your day.
Plan your day by writing a one-pager.
During my Journey, I face a problem
which seems to be small but it was
a big problem.
The problem is I do not know which
work shall I do today and which shall
I leave. In this confusion, I do
those works which are non-essential
and lost all my energy in those works.
In this way, I lost my whole day.
Once I saw a video in which an Old man
share this strategy to

Plan every day with one pager and
it helped me a lot. Now I focus
on only those things which are
essential for me.
Now how can you know that
which kind of work is essential
and which are not.
For this, I like to give a small
framework which I learned
from another youtube video.
There are four types of works
1. Which are essential and to be
done on a priority basis
2. Which are essential but can be
done today or tomorrow
3. Work which you can do or leave.
Does not matter.
Leave these kinds of work.
4. Which were not essential still
you wasted your energy on the work.
Leave this work now.
Now write the first and second type of work
on one pager and spent your day in the
same way. In this way, you will remain focused
for the complete day. Your day will remain Productive.
If someone needs your help and it is very essential
to help him/her then I recommend to
leave all your work on that day so that
you can remain focused to help him/her.
But remember time is money.
So, these kinds of days shall be less
in your life.
The final thing is the clarity break.

What mistake I did
I remain focused to my
work for seven days a week.
I remain less productive when
I did so. But when I start taking
clarity break for two days a week
i.e Saturday and Sunday
I became more productive.
So, In these two days, I focus
on planning only.
In this way, I remain laser sharp
and focused on Just one thing
and it increased my productivity.
And If I can do it anyone can
do this because I am less
intelligent than an average person.
I know and accept this reality.
It is not bad. This is the gift of nature
over which we have no control.

VIII

Reverse

What I observed and learn in daily life is the
the reverse of the formula of success.
Even when I started my Journey I did the same.
What people think is
"I want to earn a lot of Money"
which is the result.
But they have no identity, no process to do so.
Just a desire i.e they are desire-centric people.
So, they fail until and unless they achieve
the correct identity and correct process.
If they did not achieve the correct identity
and process then they will never
achieve their desired result.
But if somehow they achieve the
desired result due to any reason then
then it may be very dangerous for them.
In other words, if people have
direction *Result-Process-identity*
It may be dangerous for them.
Let us see some examples to understand it.

Suppose, Someone wants to earn a lot of money
He will fail because he has no identity, no process.
No one will pay him because
he wants to earn a lot of money.
Still, he wants to earn a lot of money.
What is the option then?
In this way, many anti-social
elements come into existence.
They get money quickly and in this way,
they spoil their own life.
Many times I predicted about
some people that they will
face financial burden.
After, Some months it really happens.
Just because they want money
and somehow they get money.
But if they develop that much capacity.
i.e they create a correct identity and
the process then they can reach
to their desired result easily.
Let us take another example
I lift 130 kg in the gym four days a week.
If someone wants to lift 130 kg what will happen?
He is not an Athlete, not a gymmer.
He doesn't do regular workouts.
Still, if he lifts 130 kg somehow.
It may be very dangerous for him.
Even many gymmer who do
regular workouts hesitate to do so
because they do not have that capacity right now.
Once they achieve that capacity then it will
be a normal routine activity for them.
In this way, I reached a new framework.

If you want to achieve a result and achieved
it then it may be dangerous for you
because you may not be capable
to achieve and retain it.
But if you focus on identity and
the process then slowly you acquire
capacity and then you can achieve
your desired result easily and
enjoy it for a lifetime.
Again I like to say focus on
Identity-Process-Result
In this way, you will reach the result
with minimum time and effort.
And it is never too late.
If you started your journey
just follow this formula.
You will achieve amazing
results which will shock you.
So, One more thing which I like to say
"Work of the player is to play the game,
not to win or lose the game"
What generally people think about
rich people are also opposite to
what is reality?
People think that being rich people
means a lot of luxury and liability.
But in real rich people are very simple.
They invest most of their money
and manage their expenses with savings.
Whereas, Poor people invest
only if they have some savings.
So here is a small framework which
will transform your life.

Expenses = investment
Savings = your requirements
In my life after many years
I understand one more thing
which is going to change your
life and business.
Poor people focus on big things.
Rich people focus on small things.
Small things are more important
then big things, because small
things integrate to create big things.
A Series of small events integrate to
create big events.
For example:
Anyone is alcoholic. Why?
It is because one day he
drink alcohol just because
their friends forced him.
Today he is an alcoholic.
What if we did not allow
this one day to come into our life?
We will never become alcoholics.
What if we can end the identity of
alcohol inside our inner world?
We can leave the habit of drinking.
What Poor people do, they focus on
The problem when it is next to
impossible to solve the problem.
People understand importance
of the team only when they fail
for the first time.
Then they recognize that behind
any successful business team

is very important.
Earning the first million is harder than
earning the first one hundred million.
So, From today please start focusing
on small things. It will transform your
life forever.
Poor people focus on problems
when it is very big and next to
impossible to solve. Hence they keep
on struggling for a lifetime.
Still, they think that money is
their problem.

IX

Team

I learn from my own experience during the Journey.
   When I try to hire team members
   I face huge trouble because the company
   was new. What if he worked and
   did not get his salary etc. There are
   many more questions like this.
   Even if someone, this person may not have
   the fundamentals that my organization needs.
   So, when you are at step zero
   no one like to work with you.
   You will face huge trouble hiring team members.
   You may face trouble paying them
   due to a lack of Revenue.
   It will increase the financial burden as well.
   But still, you need a team who can work for you.
   Further, Various activities are involved in the business.
   You need to look after-

- Company incorporation
- Mission of organization

- Law
- Management
- Marketing
- Sales
- Compliance
- Fundraising
- Customer service
- Human Resource
- Accounts
- Customer retention
- R&D
- Product development etc

and many more things
but you cannot do this alone.
You cannot do it yourself.
But when I left no stone
unturned what I observed was Amazing.
When I was preparing for Defence Services,
One CA was living in the same building.
When I asked for help, He helped
I with accounts return filing, etc.
When I asked for help from
another school friend who is a developer
he helped me with technology.
He systems which are very important for me.
And they take nothing from me.
They Just help me in their own area of specialization.
So, who will be your team?
You need a team with minimum operational costs.
Three kinds of people will help you in this situation
1. Your close friends
2. Interns

3. Freelancers/Self-employed people.
But you need to keep the following things in mind
your friends have their own life their own problems.
your friends may help you often but not on regular basis.
People will help you only in their area of specialization.
Only your close friends will help you for free
Never forget to praise your friends in your friend circle.
Never forget to thank your friends.
Self-employed people work for money so you have to pay them for their work.
Outsource your non-core business to them.
Interns are people who want to learn "How to work"
You have to train them and give stiffen every month.
*In 2017 I learn one thing which is very helpful for me and you as well, Outsourcing increases efficiency and reduces costs.

X

Investment

In this chapter, you are going to learn the difference between investment of the rich and poor.

If you invest in the investment of the rich, you will be rich.

If you invest in the investment of poor, you will be poor.

Investment of Poor

1. FD
2. RD
3. Life insurance
4. Mutual Fund
5. Pension Funds etc
6. Bonds
7. Shares from the share market

Investment of Rich

- *Health*: Health is the first investment of a rich person.

If you are healthy, If are energetic, If you never get tired then it will be a win-win situation for you.

So, I recommend investing in your health first.

One hour of workout five to six days a week is enough.
You can do any type of workout or exercise
but consistency is important.
***Please do not take it casually.**

- *Start new companies(At step Zero)*
- *Private Placement*
- *Convertible notes*
- *Private Equity*
- *Limited Partners*
- *Real estate syndicate*
- *Pre IPO*
- *Sub Prime Finance*
- *Gold*
- *Silver etc*

Many times you may listen that there must be diversification

in Investment. I completely disagree with this statement.

Please ask these kinds of people" how much money
you earned using this method "?

Personally, I never saw any such data which
proves that this statement is true.

What I learned from my two mentors.

Words are different but expressions were the same.

What they try to say is

"your investment shall be laser-focused"

In other words, "you shall focus on a single source of Income".

You shall invest that income to create another source of Income.

But you shall focus on a single source of income.

Even in my routine life, I observed that when
People focus on more than one source of Income
their income gets reduced.
So from today focus on a single source of Income.
Then invest that income to create another source of Income.
Business and investing shall be a Plan.
A Very simple plan.
Let me share one plan of mine.
I want to write one book that people
shall get crazy to get that book.
After reading that book they shall become my raving fan.
That's all I want to do.

XI

Assets

What problem people face is they want a lot of Money.
But money is a trap.
It cannot make you rich.
Yes, Money is a trap.
It will never make you rich.
Then what makes rich people rich is Assets?
So, what is the first asset at step zero?
It is you.
You are the first asset
you are the first liability.
If you are an asset you will create assets.
If you are a liability you will create liabilities.
When I started my Journey.
I do not have money.
Banks did not give me loans.
Investors did not give me funding.
What I did.
I learned marketing.
Now I do not need money to build businesses.
Do you know From where did I get this idea ?

From my first mentor.
So, Mentors are very important in our Journey.
When you learn how to create a business with a good system
you can easily start and run any business.
Everyone has their own strategy.
So, In this way when we became assets, we start creating assets.
But I have seen many people who buy land
Pay taxes on that land year on year
but never earn from that land.
Now, This is a pure liability.
This does not mean the land is a liability.
The buyer of the land is a liability.
He paid the cost of land from his own pocket.
Then he paid taxes from his own pocket.
In this way, he tendered a huge amount of money
to others. Finally, he has to sell this land in need of money
at a lower price. Still, he will tell that not having money
is his problem.
So, you are the liability and you are the asset.
It does not matter whether you have money or not.
If you are an asset you will create assets and go rich.
At the beginning of the Journey, everyone is a liability.
Hence, we face loss in the beginning.
This is not loss.
This is the investment in yourself.
That is why Entrepreneur does not worry
about these kinds of Losses.
Let us understand the types of Income
This will help you a lot in your journey.
There are three types of Income

1. Earned Income

2. Portfolio Income

3. Passive Income

1. Earned Income: This is the Income on which most people focus.

This is the income that you get by working actively.

If you do not work you will not earn.

Example: Salary, Incentive, Bonus, etc.

2. Portfolio Income: This income is Just like capital gains.

For example: If you purchase something for Just 10 Bucks and

Sold it in 15 Bucks. You get a profit of 5 Bucks.

This is simply Portfolio Income.

3. Passive Income: This is the kind of Income you are earning even if you are not working.

You just made effort for one time and get earning for a lifetime.

Example: Royalty, Dividend, Rental Income, etc

Rich people focus on

Portfolio+Passive Income

Passive Income

Portfolio Income

whereas poor people focus only on earned Income only.

XII
Recession

For years I was looking answers
of this question
"How businesses survive
during a recession ?"
This is because you need to think
and design your business in
the such way that it can survive
during adverse times.
I did not get the answer to this question.
But what I get is better than
the answer to this question.
Businesses can grow during a recession.
This growth will be exponential
if you know the correct way.
So, Let us understand how.
There are two methods to do so
which I learned from my two mentors.
First Method
Let me share a small story.
There was a person who live in

a small village during ancient times.
At that time people were looking
for gold.
one day the person found an ore
of gold in the river which
was flowing through the river.
The person gives information
about this to villagers that
"gold is in the river".
Then people decided to dig the
river to get gold. The person did not
dig the river, instead of that, he
opened a store in which he sold
the equipment required to dig the river.
In this way, he became the first millionaire
in that village.
You can do the same.
when a recession starts, more companies
and firms come into existence.
If you can help them with the equipment
required to grow their business
you will grow faster than them.
This is how Hosting companies,
Banking companies etc grow
exponentially during a recession.
They provide equipment to businesses
which helps businesses to grow.

Second Method

During a recession those companies
who face financial stress are acquired
by Businesses that have surplus cash
or Assets Companies who file bankcurrupcy
are acquired by other companies

with surplus cash.
During a recession and economic slowdown
when prices of everything go down then
Companies that have surplus cash
buy them or Companies/People
having good knowledge acquire them
using debt.
When bad days end.
These assets acquire by businesses
give them good returns.
But beware, Do not go with
second method without
enough knowledge.
Otherwise, it may go against you.

XIII

Secrets

Now I am going to share a big secrets which
is hard to except but when you will
except your life will become easier.
I learned this concept when I was
learning copywriting.
What I learned is
*People are selfish, they think about
themself, not about you.*
Initially, I excepted this reality partially.
I was thinking that everyone is not selfish.
Some people are selfish, some are not.
With time realize that this concept
is applicable to everyone
except for family members.
With time I understand that it is applicable
on my family members as well.
But, it's ok. For our parents,brother-sisters,
for every family member, I can bear this.
I learned one more concept in
another course which is

harder to accept. But when I observed
the world I understand this concept.
When I combine these two concepts
the new concept that I get give correct
definition of the world.
This entire world is brutal, cruel, and selfish.
Everyone thinks about themself.
No one thinks about you.
Everyone for himself.
This is a very harsh reality.
But when you will recognize
this reality your life will become easier.
It may take years for you to accept this reality.
But you will realize it today or tomorrow.
So, Please realize this harsh reality.
Before taking any decision I keep
this concept in my mind.
It helps me a lot in day-to-day life.
Yes, A few exceptions are there.
But you will not be able to
survive with help of exceptions
because they are very limited
in numbers.
When I started my first youtube channel
I requested thousands of people
to subscribe to my youtube channel
but only 29 people subscribed
to the channel.28 out of 29 were my family
members or friends. They subscribed
to maintain a good relationship with me.
It means only one out of thousands
of people subscribed.
It does not require money to

subscribe to any youtube channel
still, I get just one subscriber.
Why? Now I recognize why they
did not subscribe.
During adverse times no one will be with you.
But when you succeed, the world will be with you.
This is why I do not bother about what
People are saying. Whatever they say
It is meaning less to me just
because I am successful they are with me
and they will not even receive my call
if I need their help.
The day you have money they will
treat you like a king but when they
recognize you are in trouble
they will not even talk with you.
Next time anyone tries to demoralize
you remember their word has no meaning.
They are demoralizing you
because they know you do not
have money. They want to show you
that they are superior to you and
if the behavior of someone changes
with your situation, it doesn't mean
that you shall change your behavior
in the same manner.
Be humble to everyone. Respect everyone.
They have sacrificed their *conscience.*
They are salve of money, you are not.
You will never sacrifice your *Conscience.*
You are not a slave of money.
This is also a problem people have in them.
They *Conscience* . They are ready to sell their *Conscience.*

They are ready to sacrifice their *Conscience*.
But you are not ready to sell your *Conscience*.
You are notgoing to sacrifice your *Conscience*.
This is why you will grow in your life.
You are an Entrepreneur.
Your work is to build a business,
not to earn a lot of money.
you will huge earn money
but as a side product.
(You will re-invest it to grow further)
I am an Author.
My work is to avail information to
my readers which can add value
in their life and business.
Not to earn a lot of money.
Money is just a side product.
I may get results, but I may not get results.
But I will continue the process.
I will continue writing books to help my readers.
I am the founder of Excellloans Pvt Ltd.
So, I will work on behalf of my company.
My company needs profit to continue its mission.
I do not take any salary from the company.
Still, I work with dedication because
I am an Entrepreneur, Founder of the Company.
My work is to build the business.
Not to earn a lot of Money.
I am doing this since childhood.
This is why I learn everything
three times faster than an average person.
My heart and Soul give me 100 % Support.
I give my 100 % to whatever I do.
I feel proud in doing any work.

This is how I lift 130 kgs in Gym.
This is how I write Books with Dedication.
This is how I am working Founder of the Company.
This is how to succeed on youtube.
This is how I will create my Business Empire.
I recommend using this secret
you will feel energetic, dynamic, Proud
when you will do this.
But where shall you start from?
Start from your home.
Be a nice Son/Daughter.
Be a nice Brother/Sister.
Be a nice better half.
Be a nice Father/Mother.
When you will get small success
then you will automatically
implement it in your business.
Remember, you will not get
success instantly. It takes time.
Remember you are person with
high commercial value.
Future of your country and society
is in your hand.
Today you may be at zero.
tommorow you will be at Millions.
After some years you will be at Billions.
If you loose millions of people will bear
the cost.If you suceed millions of people
will get benefit from that.
So,Leave no stone unturned to be sucessfull.
with these words I like to invite you
to community of **insider investors
and Rock this world with your presence.**

XIV

youtube marketing

I am going to share my book Organic leads secrets or
Free Traffic so that you can use this to market your business.
But please do not start it until you have a stable source of Income
and your business crossed revenue of first million.
I invested two years and ten moths of struggle to suceed
in youtube.I hope you will suceed faster than me.
This book is dedicated to people who want to start a new business or
have just started a business. This book will help them to generate leads
for their business which is essential for every business. I personally face
this problem during the first year of my business and I don't want that every
new Entrepreneur/business owner shall meet the same problem.
I got the solution and I like to give this solution to my future customers.

In the future, If you need any kind of Loan then please feel free to contact us.

*Youtube channel is itself a business now.

15.

Foreword

After Covid ads cost of all social media platforms and search engines are increasing. It is not a new thing.

In the past also they increase their ad costs to make more profit.

Their ultimate goal is to earn more and more money

through ads. They don't think for you. They want that

you shall invest the maximum money in the ads through them.

The reality is that 80 % of the money you will invest in paid ads will give no return.

Customers you acquire through Paid ads may not be a quality customer.

They may not purchase high-ticket products/services from you.

They may not be interested to have a long-term relationship with your business. So what other options are valid to grow your business?

Especially, if your business is small right now.

The only way is to reduce your cost per lead(CPL) to zero. In other words, acquire customers with organic methods.

Now imagine, If your CPL is Zero.

How many leads you may generate?

The answer is infinite.

This means you can increase your customer base by infinite times.

you can scale your business up to infinite times.
This is how big companies became big.
There are various methods to do so.
But in this book, we learn to use youtube to generate leads.
We will learn more methods in the next series of this book.

Acknowledgments

I like to thank Mr. Kulwant nagi and Mrs. Marley Jaxx for their time, effort, cooperation,

and help. Without their help, it was quite hard for me to write this book.

I have taken their consent before mentioning their name and their

content in the book to avoid any kind of inconvenience in the future.

Special thanks to the team of Excellloans Pvt Ltd for their help and support.

CHAPTER ONE

Content

1.
Transformation
2.
The Beginning
3.
Phases
4.
Production
Topic Selection
Keyword Research
Google Keyword Research
Youtube Search Tab
Script Creation
Video Creation
5.

CHAPTER TWO

Transformation

I read this from the book Atomic Habits by Mr. James Clear.

There are three layers of behavior change

1. Outcome(changing result)

2. Process(changing habits and systems)

3. Identity(changing beliefs)

There are two ways to do anything in your life

1-2-3

i.e Outcome -Process-Identity

3-2-1

Identity-Process-Outcome
Both ways are good but the problem is direction.
If you choose identity-process-outcome then
you can achieve anything in less time and effort.
Maximum people choose outcome-process-Identity
they never change processes and beliefs.
Finally, they conclude that these things do not work etc etc.

So the very first thing change your identity.
Consider yourself a YouTuber from today.
Now, what is the process?
Create content and upload content that is helpful for
your audience at a fixed interval of time.

optimize your video in such a way that it shall reach your audience.

Improve your content day by day, Month by month, and Year by year.

If you did it then you don't need to worry about the result.

You will automatically get the result.
If you did this 90 % of your work is done.
I will share the remaining strategy which worked for me.

When I started working on my youtube channel again
I used the same strategy and my 5th video ranked on rank 1

on three keywords. Due to this one-ranked video, my channel

started getting more views. I got my first sale just after
uploading the second video. But I am interested in the Process

and my beliefs. In less than a month my video ranked on 1st rank on three keywords.

And if I can do it then anyone can do this by following the same process which I am going to share in this book.

I will share everything which I did and which worked for me.

Remember, the work of the player is not to win the game.

The work of the Player is to play the game and improve it every day.

CHAPTER THREE

The Beginning

This is the time when I started my company Excellloans Pvt Ltd.

I was facing problems getting customers.

Then I realize that this Market is very competitive.

With time I realize that not only this market is competitive but

every market is competitive. So no matter what business I do

It will be competitive.

I am an Ex banker who started my carrier in Banking on the 8th of Feb 2017

as a sales officer or you may say a sales executive.

It was a hard-core sales job and my job was to acquire customers

from the open market. Companies and firms were my targeted customer.

So I decided to serve the same customer base again.

During that time I learned one thing which is very helpful for me still.

"If you are not getting results then something is wrong in your process"

So I understand that something is wrong with my Process.

Once Mr. Kulwant nagi suggested I create content on any Platform for

In 4-6 Months then I will start getting customers.

I was very impressed by his polite and simple behavior.

He is the founder of Blogging cage and Affiliate booster with

an income of eight figures. Still very polite.

I approached many people but only he gave me time to

ask some of my questions. He is a full-time affiliate marketer

hence I asked about affiliate strategies that my customers

can use to grow their businesses.

You can watch the interview on my youtube channel for free.

Below is the link for the interview

https://youtu.be/wgFSMMWkqdE

But if you have the proper knowledge and you invested money

then only you can succeed. Otherwise, your money will be at stake.

I had no knowledge about anything except Search Engine Optimisation

but It will take a good amount of time which I cannot afford right now

because time is Money. I need customers Soon.

I was trying podcasts initially but I did not get any benefit

from podcasts. Then I tried paid ads. My cost per lead was INR 600.

Now If I Acquire leads @ RS 600 then I cannot provide affordably

Product/service to customers.

Now let us think about one thing. Where is the competition?

The answer is google and Youtube.

Now why it is competitive?

Because traffic is there, Customers are there.

Now youtube and google both have Traffic.

But youtube videos may rank within a fraction of a second

if I did everything right. Hence I choose youtube first.

But I did not know how youtube works.

I learned those secrets from Ms. Marley Jaxx, CEO of YoutubeLeadMachine.

For the third time, I started working on youtube.

This time I get successful.

Now, What I think.

"If I am facing this problem then maybe many Enterprenure were facing

this problem. So let's share the solution with the maximum possible Entrepreneur"

I saw an opportunity in this problem.

CHAPTER FOUR

Phases

For easy understanding, we will divide youtube organic marketing into

four different phases -

1. Production-This is what we do before uploading any video.

2. Distribution-This is what we do after the video goes public

3. Promotion-This is what we do so that we can get more traffic on this video

4. Data analysis-This is the most significant part in which

we will analyze data from the youtube channel.

This will help you to determine KPI for your channel.

So let's understand them one by one.

CHAPTER FIVE

Production

Topic selection

Very first thing is to select the topic on which you will create content on youtube. You know your customer better than I do. So please take time to select a topic.

Until and unless you are clear about the topic do not start production.

But I can give you a small framework which will help you to take this decision.

Market---Submarket----niche

For example, In my case

Marketing-Marketing for BFSI Products-Marketing for Payment gateway.

If you need a payment gateway for your business then below

is the link to a free payment gateway cash free

Signup for free payment gateway cash free:

https://merchant.cashfree.com/merchants/ signup?referrer=partner&refCode=CFES5172

or you can get the link in the description of my youtube video.

So I will create a channel for selling payment gateway.

I will sell a payment gateway at the front end and the remaining

products/services at the back end.

The front end shall be a small ticket Product.
You must have 3-4 Products/services at the backend
to make your business Profitable.
Of course, it will take some time. you cannot do all things together.
I recommend creating one more product/service after generating
the first one million from previous products or services.
Let us take one more example to understand well
BFSI-----Loan -----Business Loan
In this way also you can select your topic.
Keyword Research
Now, what is keyword research?
Basically, you need to know what your customers are searching
for so that you can create relevant content for your customer which
is helpful for your customer.
I learned this from Ms. Marley Jaxx.
The first method is using google keyword research.
The second is using the youtube search bar.
I am going to share both methods.

Google Keyword Research

For this, you need a google ads account.
If you don't have google ads account simply create one.
The process is very simple. If you already have a google Ad account then
you can use that google ad account as well.
Simply login into your google ad account.
Click on tools and settings.
Click on the keyword planner.
Click on get search volume and forecast.
Now type your topic here.

Select a keyword idea then starts with the keyword.

Now type your selected topic in the search bar and press enter.

click on get result and see the magic of google keyword research.

Now download all keywords. You have a lot of keywords now.

But all keywords are not important to you.

Select only the relevant keywords which your customer may be searching for.

Remember to select the country in which you are doing business.

Youtube Search tab

In this method, you simply type the topic in the youtube search bar and then type "a".

note all keywords that the search tab is showing.

Then remove "a" and type "b" and so on.

keep doing this you will get a lot of keywords.

This is called the ABC technique.

Again all keywords are not relevant.

Select only those which your customers may be searching.

Now the keyword research section is over.

Script Creation

Now you need to create a script on your keyword.

If you have enough knowledge about your topic then you can

easily create your script. If not then watch the top five videos on youtube.

I recommend watching the top five videos and investing some time in knowing

more about the benefits of your product or service.

I learned during the creation of my script that your

content must have some USP which is helpful for
your customer. It must be a benefit, not a feature.
your video must have a clear agenda.

It must add some value to the life of the customer.

Try to create a hook so that people shall watch and engage.

I learned from Ms. Marley Jaxx that
you shall give a call to action during the first 20 seconds
for Subscribing to your channel and shopping small ticket-size products

because people are watching videos with full attention during this time.

when you will see my video you will find that I give a call
to action with my word as well as in writing so that
there shall be no confusion.

what I say is, "if you need a free payment gateway then the link for a free payment gateway

cash-free is in the description".Even if you are selling a low-ticket product then also

you must have something free with that product. It will increase your conversion ratio.

Like free shipping in case of a physical product, free T shit with your product, etc.

Read your script several times and during the recording video keep bullet points

in front of you but behind the camera at eye level.

I am a person who believes in experiments.

So, do experiments after learning and implementing the complete process.

Video creation
Initially when I started my first youtube channel video was not so good

in quality. I started to make the video better and better. But there was no one

to guide me the way I am guiding you. So I get a little improvement.

My face was ugly when I started my first youtube channel.

I focused on my face at that time. Then I was not comfortable speaking in front

of a camera. I was Shy to speak in front of the camera, especially when someone was around me.

But it was a need of the hour so I keep on my practice and still I am improving my performance.

If you are facing the same issues then don't worry. It happens to everyone.

The thing which changed my video quality was the anti-gravity movement.

I learned in an e-learning course that during speaking in any video

you need to do anti-gravity movements with your hands.

when I started using these tactics I saw that people like my

videos better now. Even today I use this tactic in each video.

I suggest you go to my channel and watch how I use anti-gravity

movement and it increased the quality of my video by many folds.

Below is the link to my youtube video:

https://www.youtube.com/channel/ UCZOoEhXP0dGA008VpauuGZQ

So, I recommend you use it in every video and see the magic.

During video creation, you need to focus on many more things.

Background: I use a white background so I recommend starting with the same.

Do not hesitate to do experiments. But do it later not in the beginning.

Mic: I recommend using a wired mic at the beginning with a good length

of wire so that you don't have to face any problems due to the shorter length

of wire.

Camera: The camera of your mobile is enough to record videos in the beginning.

No need to buy an expensive camera. If the camera quality of your phone is not good

then use the phone of any family member.

Camera Stand: Please take a camera stand on which the camera can be kept on an eye

label. otherwise, it will reduce the quality of the video.

Never ignore your body fitness, clothes, your beauty, or handsomeness.

Remember, If your video is beautiful everyone like to watch it.

otherwise, customers will not make any purchases from you even if it is free.

I learned in my training in Feb 2017 that 80 % of the sales depend upon your look.

So if your video is beautiful then it will help you to grow your audience.

During video recording please take care that you don't have to make

much effort on editing. It will give you a lot of relief.

the final stage is editing. I use a cracked version of editing software to edit videos.

you can also do the same or you can get a subscription to good video editing software.

keep a gap of 3 seconds at the beginning and end of the video. It will help you during editing.

keep on improving your video. you may subscribe to my youtube channel to

know what further improvements I am doing in my youtube channel.

* Lenth of Video: Lenth of your video shall be less than 5 Minutes so that

Cold customers shall see your video. Remember people who come to your video

don't know you. They will watch your video only when the length of the video shall be small.

These days people do not have much time. So you shall deliver your content in less than 5 minutes.

Warm and hot customers will also watch your video. Of course, they can invest more than 5 minutes

of time as well but you have no control over traffic from youtube. Any kind of traffic/Prospect may visit

the video. So, I recommend creating 5 minutes of video only. Create a video of more than 5 minutes only if

and only if it is very important.

I observed in my life small things make together create a huge impact. This is also applicable to

youtube videos as well. So focus on small elements of your videos.

After editing, Remember to change the name of your video. Now, what shall be the name of the video?

It will be the topic of your video. We will understand it in the distribution section but for now please keep this point in your mind.

* Keep your video unlisted

*do not add it to the playlist before releasing the video

*one last thing: deliver content with your heart.

Every time I deliver content with my heart I got a good ranking.

CHAPTER SIX

Distribution

Again I learned this from Ms. Jaxx.

Youtube is smarter than what we think and know.

When we upload a video on youtube, Youtube sees the video frame by frame.

So, youtube knows everything about the video.

This is why I recommend changing

the name of the video to the topic of the video.

Youtube process every data, even the name of the video.

Youtube SEO

Remember Youtube is a Search Engine. So we need to optimize

the video so that youtube will rank your video and show the

video to the audience who will like the content.

I will give you a simple strategy to do youtube SEO.

Let us understand the terms involved in SEO.

Click-through Rate (CTR): Percentage of people who click on your thumbnail after they see it.

Suppose 100 people see your thumbnail and 3 out of then

Click on your thumbnail then your CTR is 3%.

Bouns Rate: Suppose people reached your thumbnail on youtube.

They watch for just a few seconds and leave your video.

This is called bouns. If 20 out of 100 people do this then it is called bouns rate of 20 %.

Remember, we did keyword research in production. You shall use that in the title, tag and description.

Now you need a tool called tube buddy. Below is my affiliate link for the tool

https://www.tubebuddy.com/anujbharadwaj83

Signup with this link for its free version. The free version is enough as of now.

This is basically a chrome extension that will help you to optimize videos.

After installing it on the google chrome extension and creating a free account

go to youtube

type the keyword in the search bar on youtube

Click on the first video

wait for a few seconds

now see on the right-hand side below the fold.

you will find tags

Simply copy them

Repeat the same with the video on the second rank

now paste tags in the description and tags section of your video

you can put tags up to 500 words only

remove tags that are irrelevant

remove tags that are less relevant

when you see in the tags section that the number of words is up to 500

save your video now.

I recommend using more than one title in every video.

Remember to copy-paste tags in the title tags and description as well.

*Don't use a one-word title or tag. It will not rank or rank for just a few hours.

use tags with more than two words. Avoid highly competitive words like

Payment gateway, Business Loan, etc.

But how to find out other titles for videos?

we will learn this in data.

How youtube will distribute videos

Youtube ranking is not only the way through which youtube will

distribute your video. There are other methods also.

1. Suggested video

2. Browse Features

3. External

4. channel pages

5. Notification

6. other youtube features

7. Playlist

8. Playlist pages

9. video cards and annotations

10. End screen

What more you can do?

give a link to your playlist in the description

give a link to your videos in the description

Set up your video in Cards so that people may see your other video.

Setup your videos in Endscreen so that people shall see your other videos

*create videos that people like to consume from beginning to end.

So, if your video is not ranking in the beginning still youtube will distribute videos to more people who like to see your video.

The Secret Sauce

I tried each and everything I mentioned till now when I started my second youtube channel

Anuj Bharadwaj-Excellloans Pvt Ltd. But it worked a little and I gave up due to frustration.

When I started getting leads through paid ads and my CPL was Rs 600, I started working on

youtube again and did one thing which changed my youtube career.

This is what Ms. Jaxx shared but I ignored this piece of information.

What most people don't know about youtube.

"First 24 to 48 hours are most important after the video goes public. youtube will distribute videos to

more people if it gets more views in the first 24 to 48 hours "

So what I did this time. I purchase views for my video every time I upload a video.

I purchased 1k views. It did not perform well.

I purchased 7k views. Again It did not perform well.

I purchased 10k views. It did not perform well.

I purchased 19k views. It ranked this time. Not on rank one but on page one.

I was thinking "how can I rank my video on rank one now ?"

I did a small change again.

This time I purchased instant views and my video ranked on rank one.

Remember, Small things make a big impact.

This was how I ranked my video.

you can implement this strategy for yourself as well.

It worked for me so It will work for you as well.

So, After uploading get instant views.

Instant means just after your video goes public your video shall get starting views.

Suppose your video gets 1200 views in the first hour.

The algorithm of youtube will be in favor of your video.

your video needs views as per the competitiveness of your niche.

I got ranked in just 21k views So I did not purchase views of more than 21k

but your video may need more or less.

So, I recommend starting from 21k views and increasing it in the next videos if required.

Keep on increasing views till your video ranks. But it will work when everything is ok.

Thumbnail

In the beginning, It was quite hard for me to create the thumbnail.

What I did. I download the canvas app on my mobile.

Then I find a different kind of thumbnail.

I select a thumbnail that I found suitable.

Then I edit its content. This thumbnail achieved very poor performance.

Then I saw the thumbnail of the channels which attack the same kind

of people which I attack and create a thumbnail akin to that.

I kept my clear picture on the thumbnail so that people shall recognize me

if youtube recommends them my video again and again via the search option,

browse option suggested video or others.

One thing which helped me is the word"Ex- Banker".

I wrote this word in the thumbnail and CTR increased by 0.1 %

I am an Ex banker so I can write this in a thumbnail.

When I changed the color of this word from white to yellow then CTR again increased.

Here is what I discovered from these things.

1. your thumbnail shall have your clear beautiful pic

2. you need to give the answer to your customer in just one word-why shall they see your video?

I am an Ex banker so I wrote Ex banker. Find out yours.

Remaining things of the thumbnail.

Your thumbnail shall tell clearly what your video is about in 2-5 words.

I recommend going to my channel and creating a thumbnail akin to mine

in the canvas app. Starting is the hardest thing to do. So do what I do and do

experiments when you learn how to rank your video and other things which

I disclosed.

CHAPTER SEVEN

Promotion

I saw many times big YouTubers went to different platforms to promote them.

I was amazed that why shall they come to this platform.

They already have traffic on their youtube channel.

When they upload their video they share them on their social media handles.

I have seen many times this thing so they are doing it.

while writing this book it came to my mind that they are

promoting so that people shall see their "Master Show" i.e their youtube videos.

So, we shall also do the same. We will use different strategies to promote our youtube channel.

1. After your videos go public, create multiple 30-second videos from the videos.

Then post them on Facebook reels, Instagram reels, etc where people like to see video content.

Look for new social media

2. Lowest hanging fruits are your family and friends connected with you on social media.

Create and share your success story regularly on your social media Handle.

If there is no news then create some successful news and share it everywhere.

3. when you start earning then invest to go to big news channels etc to grow your audience.

4. when you will get traffic then collab with other influencers.

5. Think of more methods to promote your youtube channel.

CHAPTER EIGHT

Data Analysis

In today's world "data is everything".

This is true for YouTube as well.

youtube will give you some data.

tube buddy will give you some data.

Analyze those data and then decide your KPI i.e key performance indicators.

Remember I used Ex banker in the thumbnail?

CTR increased by 0.1% but how did I know?

when I changed color from white to yellow further CTR increased.

But how do I know it? The answer is data Analysis.

One more important thing which I was ignoring was data.

Let us see the broader side of data analysis.

I uploaded a video "How to get a Payment gateway"

Now let us see the data:(Different tools and devices will show different results)

Result on youtube

It is ranked among 17 Tags

Cashfree signup page 1 Rank 2

Cashfree signup page 1 Rank 3

Cashfree Page 1 Rank 8

cash free account kaisai banai Page 1 Rank 19

Best payment gateway for India Page 1 Rank 5

Payment gateway Signup Page 1 Rank 8

payment gateway Sign up Page1 Rank 9

How to get a payment gateway page 1 Rank 20

I recommend you to go and see the video about why it is ranking on

cash free signup

cash free sign up

cash free

Payment gateway signup

Payment gateway sign up

Payment gateway for India

but I made video on "How to get a payment gateway "

Now search these keywords on different devices.

you will see different rankings on different devices.

This means youtube is lessening us and observing our search Intent.

Youtube knows what the user is looking for.

The ranking is low for "How to get a payment gateway"

and high for "cashfree signup and cashfree sign up"

because those customers who reach to video using the keyword

cashfree signup and Cashfree sign up watched this video are more satisfied.

They may invest more time than people who reached to video with the keyword

How to get a payment gateway.

In the video, I explained the signup process of Cashfree but the title was How to get a payment gateway.

you will see in every video that the ranking will change after 2-3 days as per the comfort of the customer.

If you see the video today you will see something different from today.

This is because of changes in the behavior patterns of customers.

I used

Cashfree signup

Cashfree sign up

Cashfree

cash free account kaisai banai

Payment gateway for India

Payment gateway Signup

payment gateway Sign up

in tag and description.

I feel something is wrong. It did not rank on the keyword on which I tried to rank.

It ranked accidentally on some keywords in the description and tags.

It means youtube consider on keyword present in the tag as well as the description.

After analyzing the complete data of this video I understand one thing which I did wrong.

I named it Align strategy.

Align strategy

In the next video, I aligned everything according to the title of the video.

I created a video on "Payment gateway documents required".

I explained clearly what documents are required for having a payment gateway account.

This time it ranked on rank 1 on

Payment gateway document required page 1 rank 1

Payment gateway document page 1 rank 4

cashfree document required page 1 rank 1

Paytm document required page 1 rank 3

This is what youtube is doing

Just after a new one is uploaded and released, Youtube gives a ranking according to keywords

that we give in the title as well as on secondary keywords present in Tags and descriptions.

Then youtube observes the performance of the video for some hours. After some hours youtube

changed the ranking of the video to the comfort of traffic. It means when

people search "Paymentgatewaydocument required"They see my video on rank one.

Now according to the number of views, CTR, Bouns rate,

watch time, etc youtube will give a ranking to videos on the keyword"payment gateway document

required".In other words, youtube gives ranking to videos according to its algorithm.

The algorithm is designed to keep people engaged on the platform for maximum time.

So, we may say content is the king but only when it reaches the Audience.

This is what we do

we upload videos and just after uploading we order instant views and likes on our video.

(views are the most important factor of the youtube algorithm)

Every second 500 hours of content is being uploaded on youtube.

So competition is very high on youtube. Hence we need to match

the algorithm of youtube with our video.

Next time when you upload a new video on youtube, Please track changes in

ranking and analyze data. You will understand what I am trying to say.

I analyze data from youtube and tube buddy many times a day.

It helped me a lot to rank my videos.

Keep on analyzing data each and every day. It will help you to understand

how you can rank videos on youtube, how to increase their distribution etc.

Maybe someday you will help out me to understand it well.

Download YT studio app right now. It will also help you a lot.

CHAPTER NINE

Ultimate goal

Do you know why companies select celebrities for their ads?

This is due to their fan base.

These days Brands approach influencers. Do you know why?

Because of their fan following.

We are doing the same thing here.

The goal of your youtube channel is to create your fab base.

The more fans you have, the more revenue your business will have.

They will even purchase products/services which they don't need.

Just because they are your fan.

Remember to maintain good relations with your fan and followers.

In the future, you will observe that you get most of your customers

are people who consumed your content.

People who consumed your content will become your partners, your Affiliate, etc.

So it will help you a lot to grow your business in the coming future.

Some words from Mr. Kulwant Nagi which he shared on Facebook

"Most of the things in life, which make you feel accomplished, take at least five years to achieve. This can include building a profitable business, having a loving relationship, getting your book published, getting in the best shape of life, raising a kid, and every big thing which makes you feel complete. Five years is a long time. It is much slower than most of us would like. If you accept the reality of slow progress, you have every reason to take action today. If you resist the reality of slow progress, five years from now you'll simply be five years older and still looking for a shortcut."

So, Simply start today. Stop looking for any shortcut.

CHAPTER TEN

Earning

There are various methods of earning from youtube.

So let us discuss the strategies through which you can make.

Monetisation

I am going to share a harsh reality with you that I learned when

I was learning copywriting.

"In this world everyone is selfish and no one thinks about you"

This is why I recommend not asking for help in the beginning.

When I asked for help from people to subscribe to my youtube channel.

I get a little conversion ratio. Only those people who love me

and care about me subscribed to the channel.

I shared my video on social media handles so that people may help me

by watching and subscribing to the channel. But the response was negative.

So, this time I know that people are not going to help me out

because they have no benefit in doing so.

Remember: If you need something, People will never give you that thing.

If they feel that you are growing even if they don't support you.

They will think that you are successful. Resistance of people will reduce.

Hence, I recommend in the Promotion phase share your success story.

Don't ask for help.

What shall you do then for Monetisation?

Buy 1100 Subscribers.

Upload the video at regular intervals.

Buy instant views for your video then share it with your

family, friends, Social media handles, etc after 48 hours when your video got the views that you ordered.

Your video is ranking on youtube now, Share this news. You get 31k views, share this news.

Don't buy watch hours. You may ask why?

Because when you buy views you will get watch time as well for free.

Suppose you buy 31k views and with every view, you get 1 minute of watch time.

So, you get 31k minutes of watch time for free.

So why not invest money in views and subscribers only and get watch time for free?

When your channel gets monetized share this news. Some people may think that you are successful.

This is why monetization is important. You are successful in the monetization of youtube.

"This is just the front end of your business" you know this. Everyone does not know this.

"You are not earning huge"You know this. Everyone doesn't know.

People have their own myths in their minds. Let them act as per their myths.

You are earning from every customer now. Even if they don't pay you anything.

Sponsorship:

If you want to get sponsorship then I recommend you wait for brands to contact you.

Just mention your email in the description of every video for business queries.

If you get sponsorship but the brand does not get business/Customers then your relationship with

brands will not be good and ultimately it will tell over your business in the long run.

So, Just wait for brands to contact you. When they contact you can negotiate on your terms.

Remember the process is important not the result. You shall make yourself capable to

give business to brands not taking sponsorship somehow.

Leads

This is our primary goal. So please stick to it from day one.

Leads are the blood of any business. If you do not have leads, It will tell over your business.

The remaining all things are secondary but leads are our primary goal.

Suppose you got some leads from youtube and converted them into sales.

you will get earnings from the first sale then from the second sale, and then from the third sale.

So, the average earnings from your sale will increase. This is more lucrative than anything else.

So, from day one focus on leads, leads, and leads. The remaining things are secondary.

Those customers who come to you are quality customers because they like you.

They are ready for a long-term relationship with you.

The average earnings from these customers will be high.

If you acquire customers through paid ads then they may not be quality customers.

They may not like to maintain long-term relationships.

They may not be ready to pay you a high price for your product or service.

Hence, customers through organic means are the best customer to deal with.

CHAPTER ELEVEN

First Fundraising

I learned this from my own experience when I was trying

to start my business for the first time.

I left no stone unturned to raise funds to start my company.

But due to covid, I get multiple failures to raise funds for my business.

Neither banks helped me out nor investors helped me to start the business.

I continued to fail for months.

Finally, my mother gave me her jewelry so that I can get money by

selling jewelry and starting my business.

Later on, I saw on the YT channel of YCommbinator

that every business does the same.

So, you are going to get funds for your first business from your family or friends.

It may be your father, mother, your elder brother, elder sister, or your close friend.

Every business does the same. It is a proven strategy to get the first fund for every business.

Remember only those people who have money or

money management skills and have love and

affection for you will do so.

You are a new Entrepreneur right now

and you have no proven track record so

no other person/Organization will be ready to invest in your business because

their money will be at high risk.

So, from today focus on people who are very close to you,

and who loves your success more than their money.

Otherwise, there is no other reason to invest in you or your Business.

This amount will be very small so you will become very creative due to this reason.

So that it is in a positive way.

One more thing which I will tell you that if you have no money and if you want to start a business, then this

is a golden opportunity for you because if you started a business even if you have no money for once then

you can do it again and again which leads to infinite returns.

Now you need no money to start any project or business because you will raise funds for that and every

time you will raise funds you will be smarter every time. That is why you are Entrepreneur.

Everyone does not have this capacity. Only Entrepreneurs have this capability. Ordinary people need

money for everything which is why they remain poor so far.

If you have money to start a business, then I recommend you not to use that money.

Keep that money and raise funds for your business.

Believe me, you will become smarter every time you raise funds for your business or project.

Even the founder of amazon raised a seed fund for his business from his parents.

I raised funds from my mother for business there are many more examples in this world like this.

So, raise funds for your business and be smarter not only for this time but for

every time you need to start any project or business.

When you will have a successful track record then everyone will be ready to give you funds. Every now knows that you are good in business and their money is safe now.

Till that time only you have to struggle for funds. So, After the first success, you will have

Surplus money on your conditions.

I will guide you in the future as well so that you can become more and more successful.

I will share my blueprints with you so that you can be successful in the least possible time.

CHAPTER TWELVE

Entrepreneur success cycle

I hear about this in a weekly master class of a course for the first time, but I didn't believe the concept.

After six months of starting the first company "Excellloans Pvt Ltd," I was trying to diagnose why my

business is not growing.

During that time again I reached the same concept. This time a successful Entrepreneur and marketer.

And there is no reason to not believe him. Then I understood the problem.

My business was not working according to this system called the Entrepreneur success cycle.

So, I implemented this system in my business. Currently, it is in the implementation stage.

So now I am going to share with you this entrepreneur success cycle and recommend

you use this system in your business.

It works for all kinds of businesses so you do not need to think that it will work for your business or not.

It will work for every business.

Stage 1: Attraction

This is the first stage of every business.

In this stage, we attract customers to our business. We make our client or customer base in this stage.

The cost of the customer acquisition shall be zero. Create organic methods to acquire customers.

You are an entrepreneur be creative and think out of the box.

This will help you to scale your business faster with time you will understand its value.

Right now, just think from today onwards that how you can acquire customers by organic means.

I recommend creating one product for this stage and the give the most valuable piece to that product.

It shall be a small ticket-size product.

Remember you shall not move to the next step until you earned one million at least and created a pipeline

to earn clients/customers for your business. Also, create a long-term relationship with that customer so

that you can earn more from the same customer again and again.

Let's understand this with an example.

If I want to sell this book, I will share the most valuable chapter of this book.

If I want to sell a bike, then I will create an info product related to safe riding.

If I want to sell a saree, then I will create an info product related to that which shall be very valuable for

women and recommend my saree to those women who register for that.

Step 2: Retention

In this second step, you will cross-sell to those who purchased the first product or Info Product.

Now you have not invested to acquire customers so whatever you will earn will give you excess profit to grow your business.

Remember to maintain a good relationship with your customer to sell them at this stage.

In this retention stage, you will sell a high-ticket product to the customer and Some of them will purchase,

and you will get excess earnings to grow further.

Remember that all those who will purchase the first piece of product/info product will not purchase your

first Product and all those who purchase the first product will not purchase the second product.

Only some people will purchase the next product and the next product shall be more valuable and higher in

price next time. Once again you earn one million in this stage then move to the next stage.

Step 3: Optimisation

In this stage, you will optimize everything. For everything which is not working well or not so well you will

optimize that. This stage is very critical and essential you will understand this in the next step.

For this time just remember to optimize your business.

check things that are working well which are not and those which are not on basis of data.

Do not engage in guesswork.

Whatever data is saying is correct. Remember data never tell lie.

It is key guidance.

Let us take some examples 1000 people are coming on the website every month and

if the conversion ratio is below 2% to 5% then something is wrong.

If the conversion ratio of your lead is less than 31% then something is not good.

You need to diagnose the problem.

Now my Business is in the attraction phase.

These are just examples there are many things to optimize So keep on optimizing.

People who have no prior experience will tell you many things but neither lesson to them nor tell them

these things because these systems and ideas are worthless to them.

They will not even try to understand these concepts because they are not Entrepreneurs.

You are Entrepreneur.

*** These first three steps are most critical for new businesses.

Step 4: Systemization

Now let us understand why optimization is important.

Suppose something is wrong and can you systemise something which is not working?

The answer is no, You cannot.

So, after optimization, you will systemize the business.

This is why some businesses grow and scale and some remain small

after years because businesses systemize themself.

Now create different systems which can run the business.

Remember efficiency of a system is higher than any human as

the efficiency of the system does not reduce ever.

There are different types of systems.

System for Recruitment. System for Training

System for Customer acquisition of customers.

System for customer support etc.

Step 5: Delegation

In this stage, you appoint HOD for every department.

Now HOD of every department is responsible for that department and you are delegating them.

Let us see some examples.

HOD for HR

HOD for Marketing HOD for Sales HOD for customer service etc.

Remember there shall be only one HOD for one department.

If two people are responsible for one department then the efficiency

of that department will reduce hence only one HOD for one department.

Now give a number to every HOD. Their target will be to achieve the number.

For example, have you ever given a rating for customer service or something else?

This is the target for the customer service department to achieve a specific rating.

This is a specific number this department has to archive in terms of rating.

In the same way, you will give a specific number to every department to achieve every month.

Please remember to have a clear governance chart of your Business from the beginning.

Step 6: Automation

In this step, you will make businesses so efficient that they will run automatically.

Even if you leave the business for years it will continue to run automatically.

Now you can appoint your second in command who will replace you and either you involved in those

pieces of business which are key for an exponential jump, starting a new business or taking retirement.

As a capitalist, I like to start a new business.

Have you ever heard companies hire a CEO& MD/Vice president etc.?

They may be second in command in any company.

If you don't know then no need to worry. You will understand when you reach this stage.

Step 7: Expansion

Now your business is ready to expand. The good thing is that it will grow year after year,

Month on Month continuously It will expand without much effort now.

Congratulations, on reading this complete journey.

CHAPTER THIRTEEN

Real Business

Business is not about the outer world. It is about your inner world.

Your self-doubts, your confusion, your confidence, your leadership skills, etc.

Business and investing are team sports. You cannot do it alone.

There are three kinds of people in business

Executive, Manager(Integrator), and visionary or Entrepreneur.

Your business will not grow until you have these three kinds of people in business

You have to struggle until you transform into an entrepreneur.

It takes 3 years to complete the transformation.

The First 3 stages of a business are critical.

The first three businesses are critical.

Learn to remain comfortable in an uncomfortable situation.

You will face different challenges and problems every day in the Business world.

See what successful businesses are doing and hack their strategy and tactics to succeed fast.

To succeed fast fail. Never hesitate to fail. Fail fast and learn from that failure.

Failure is the best teacher. Believe me when you think you are growing beware.

Forget whatever you learn in traditional education. That education is of no use in Business.

Traditional education is created so that we don't have to face a scarcity of Employees. Education of

An entrepreneur is different from Traditional education.

We learn from mistakes, books, coaches, consultants, team members, attorneys, Accountants, etc.

Since childhood, our parents, society, teacher, and everyone trained us to think that mistakes = Bad, Punishment, Pain, etc. (one or all). Delete this thing from your mind.

To succeed once you must fail multiple times. Keep on trying even after multiple failures.

Someday, some week or some month you will see that your business is growing and you achieve success.

You are the asset, and you are the liability.

You are responsible for each and everything which you are facing. No one else.

If you blame someone then you will not be able to grow.

Invest in your education

Never take a Paycheck or salary from your Business.

Remember, an Entrepreneur works for free.

*Most important thing which I like to share is "Business is an Art"

It works on Proved systems and Processes.

So you need to find out and understand that proven system.

Then simply implement it in your business.

CHAPTER FOURTEEN

The secret behind helping customers

I saw many people who do not want to help their customers to be successful.

They want to keep their secrets undisclosed.

They just want to earn money from their customers.

I don't know why. Here is why I like to help my customers.

I promote a payment gateway so that I can earn recurring income.

I want to earn as much as possible.

But my customers do not want a payment gateway.

They want to acquire more and more customers.

They want maximum revenue.

If I help them to acquire leads for free, they will collect more payments

through the payment gateway. Hence my earnings will increase.

Suppose I want to sell e-learning courses to my customers.

They are earning five lakh per month.

Can they buy my course for Rs 999?

The answer is yes. They can if they trust me.

But if their earnings are Zero.

Can I sell them a course worth Rs 999?

The answer is no.

Hence, I like to help my customers to earn more so that I can earn more.

If my customers grow, I can grow easily.

If my customer does not grow, my business will struggle and finally, I will be in financial trouble.

So, I like to help my customers as much as possible.

If they grow I will automatically grow.

Finally, I request you help your customers to achieve their desire.

This is the only way for you to grow and increase earnings.

It will be helpful for you and your customers as well.

If you are an affiliate marketer then sign up 30-day free trail

of affiliate boosters and try to understand how businesses

help their customers to grow.

below is the link for the affiliate booster

https://www.affiliatebooster.com/?ref=864

CHAPTER FIFTEEN

Ideal Customer life cycle

There are seven stages of a customer life cycle in any Business.

Here your youtube channel is your business.

So it is applicable to your business as well

1. Know

2. Like

3. Trust

4. Try

5. Buy

6. Repeat

7.Refer

CHAPTER SIXTEEN

Message for Readers

I hope you enjoyed reading this book.

But your real education will start when you will start implementing

the tactics which I shared with you. I recommend reading

this book three times to take maximum benefit.

If you have any feedback or complaints then please share them with us.

Send your feedback or complaint this email

at anuj@excellloans.in with the subject "feedback or complaints"

We welcome complaints or feedback.

Please read my other book DSA Secrets

Signup for free payment gateway cash free:

https://merchant.cashfree.com/merchants/signup?referrer=partner&refCode=CFES5172

Link for our websites: https://excellloans.in/ https://excellloans.com/

Link for affiliate booster:https://www.affiliatebooster.com/?ref=864

Recommended Hosting Hostinger:https://www.hostg.xyz/SH60V

Follow me on social media

Facebook: https://www.facebook.com/anuj.bharadwaj.775/

LinkedIn: www.linkedin.com/in/anujbharadwaj

Instagram: https://www.instagram.com/anujbharadwaj83

All links are available in the description of my youtube videos.

*I buy views from followers India

If you like to be our permanent client then, please

email us at anuj@excellloans.in with the headline #Permanent Client.

Final Word

We are looking for Joint ventures so that we can grow together.

So, If you are interested to work together then, please send us an email at anuj@excellloans.in headline shall be #JV

Alternate Email Id: excellloans@gmail.com

Stay In Touch

This is series 1 of organic leads secret.

In the future, I will write series 2,3 and..... (and some other books as well.)

which will give you my proven step-by-step strategy

to acquire customers with organic means.

I am a full-time writer so often I write books.

Enjoy your reading.

Stay in touch through my youtube channel Anuj Bharadwaj -Excellloans Pvt Ltd

Link for my youtube channel

https://www.youtube.com/channel/UCZOoEhXP0dGA008VpauuGZQ

This will help you to grow your youtube channel as well.

I hope this is the beginning of our relationship.

with Thanks

Anuj Bharadwaj

Author, Founder of Excellloans Pvt Ltd